Richard Unglik

ADVENTURES IN HISTORY

Walter Foster
Jr.

In the Beginning

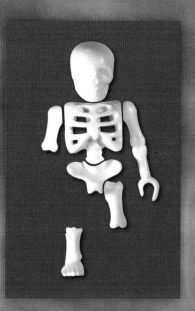

The Earth and the universe are billions of years old. In comparison, humans haven't been around very long. Lucy, one of the oldest humans we know about, lived about 3 million years ago in Africa—let's call her a "Playmopithecus."

Playmo africanus

Playmopithecus   Playmo habilis   Playmo erectus

Down from the trees, these new arrivals to the ground would go on to conquer the world. First, Playmopithecus stood up to walk on two legs. Then Playmo habilis discovered how to use stones as tools. Playmo erectus learned how to control fire, and finally playmo sapiens appeared. A group of sapiens—the Playmo neanderthalensis—disappeared long ago, and were replaced by the sapiens sapiens—US!

Playmo Sapiens

Playmo Sapiens Sapiens

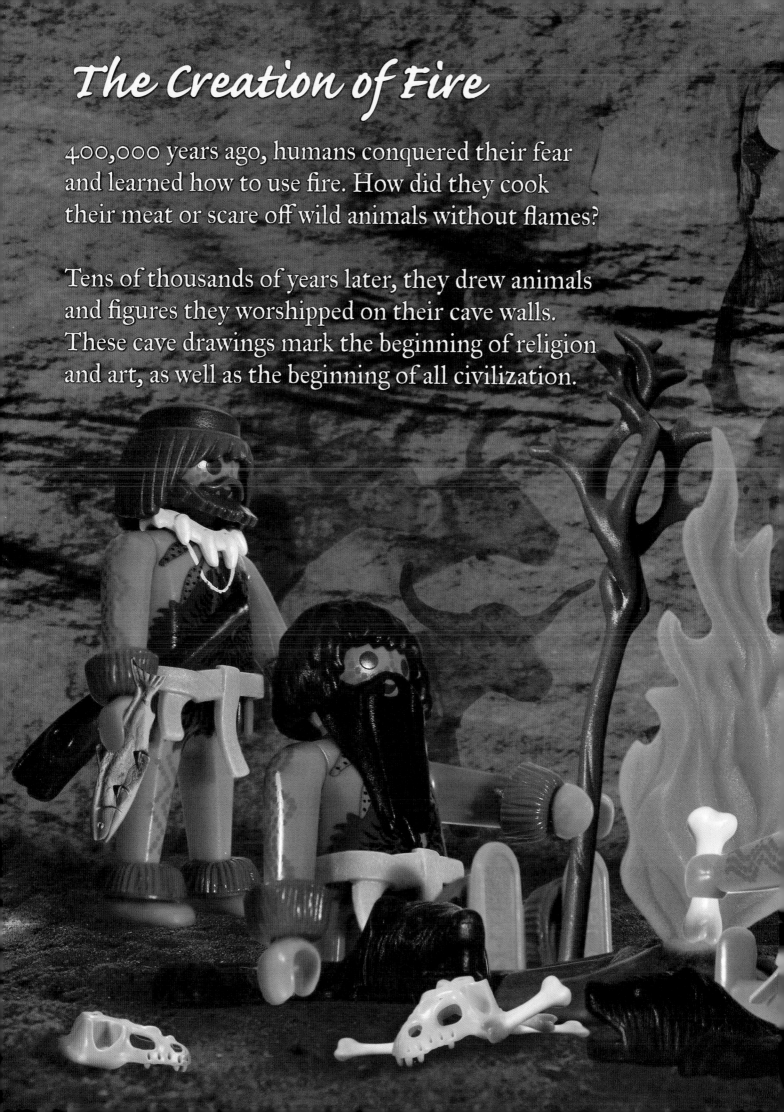

The Creation of Fire

400,000 years ago, humans conquered their fear and learned how to use fire. How did they cook their meat or scare off wild animals without flames?

Tens of thousands of years later, they drew animals and figures they worshipped on their cave walls. These cave drawings mark the beginning of religion and art, as well as the beginning of all civilization.

The Dawn of History

Since humans appeared on earth four million years ago, they have always been eager to keep evolving and progressing. Starting from the heart of Africa, humanity spread to Asia, Europe, and later, America. Nomads at heart, humans moved from one region to the next based on the availability of plants to gather and animals to hunt.

The evolution from a simple club to iron weapons and tools improved humans' ability to hunt and fight.

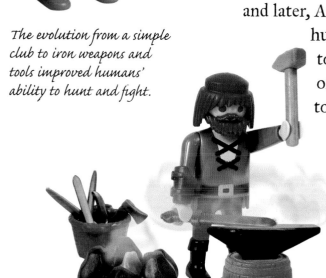

As centuries passed, weapons and tools became more advanced. Stones and simple clubs evolved into wooden spears, flint knives, harpoons, and later, bows and arrows. Humans discovered how to work with metal and invented the wheel—a true revolution! In the Neolithic period (in Europe around 6,000 BC), agriculture and farming were born. People settled in villages surrounded by wheat fields and herds of horses, sheep, and domesticated pigs.

At the end of the Neolithic era, dog became man's best friend.

There are thousands of Egyptian gods, all half-human, half-animal. The sun-god Ra is thought to be the father of all Pharaohs that reigned.

Drawings, and more stylized pictograms, were the basis for all writing until the Phoenicians invented the first real alphabet.

From Men and From Gods

On the banks of the largest rivers—the Nile in Egypt and the Euphrates and the Tigris in Mesopotamia—the first civilizations grew due to easier access to food and shelter. The invention of writing (around 3,500 BC in Mesopotamia) allowed people to record their history, while the conception of gods (both terrible and cruel and kind and protective) provided a way of understanding the origin and meaning of life.

Less than 3,000 years ago, the Phoenicians, the Cretans, and the Greeks blossomed around the Mediterranean Sea. In large cities like Athens and Corinth, people laid the foundations for astronomy, physics, mathematics, and philosophy, and citizens held the first elections in history.

Meanwhile, in Asia around 500 BC, Confucius taught of a young Indian prince, Siddhartha, who gave up his life of luxury and pleasure to meditate. He would later be known by the name Buddha.

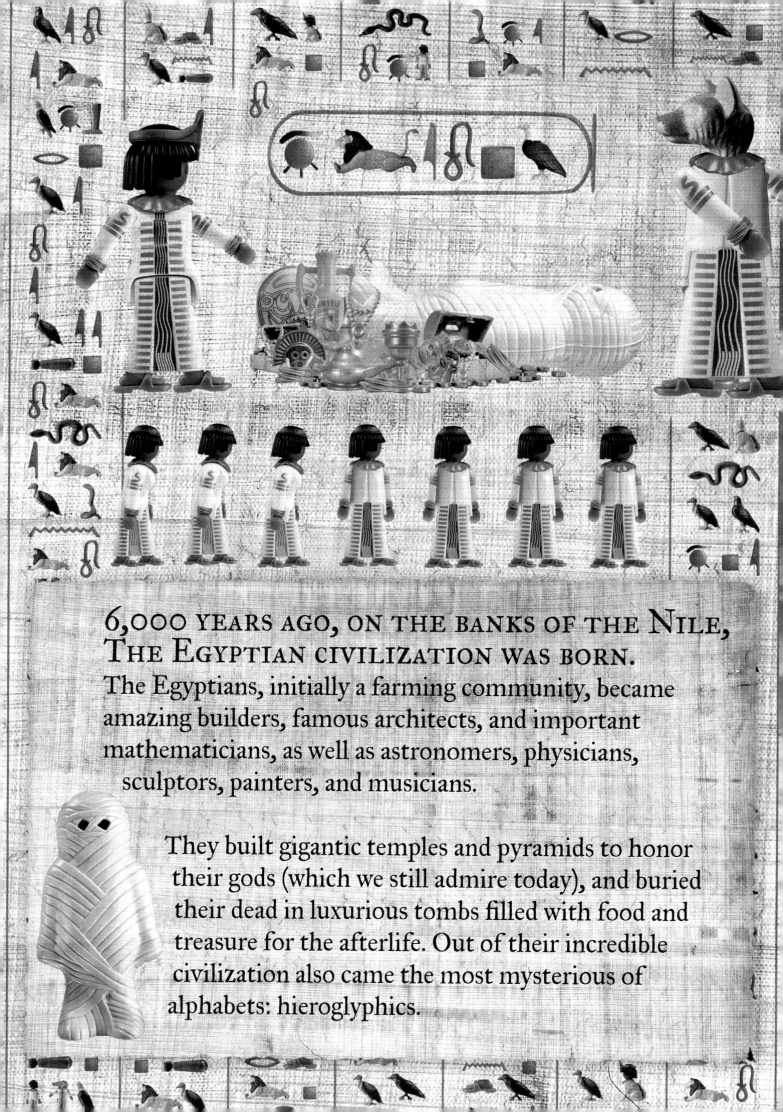

6,000 YEARS AGO, ON THE BANKS OF THE NILE, THE EGYPTIAN CIVILIZATION WAS BORN.

The Egyptians, initially a farming community, became amazing builders, famous architects, and important mathematicians, as well as astronomers, physicians, sculptors, painters, and musicians.

They built gigantic temples and pyramids to honor their gods (which we still admire today), and buried their dead in luxurious tombs filled with food and treasure for the afterlife. Out of their incredible civilization also came the most mysterious of alphabets: hieroglyphics.

Moses,
THE CHILD OF THE NILE

Over 3,000 years ago, the Egyptian Pharaoh ordered to kill all
Hebrew firstborn sons. To save her son, one Hebrew mother
hid the baby in a basket of reeds and sent it down the Nile
River. Soon afterwards, the Pharaoh's daughter discovered the
abandoned baby. Taking pity on the infant, she rescued and raised
him as her own son. She gave him the name Moses.

Moses grew up as a prince of Egypt in the Pharaoh's court. He freed his people from slavery and took them to the Promised Land, and eventually received the stone tablets of the Ten Commandments from God.

The Odyssey
The Adventures of Ulysses

The Greeks won the Trojan War thanks to Ulysses' plan to build a giant wooden horse where all of their best soldiers could hide. The Trojans brought the horse into their city, believing it to be a gift from the gods. At night, Ulysses' soldiers came out and let in the rest of the Greek army. After a few short hours, Troy was destroyed.

On their way home, the Greeks faced many dangers—it took Ulysses over ten years to reach his home island of Ithaca. Some dangers included the ferocious Cyclops, the dangerously alluring sirens, the charming nymph Calypso, and the magical Circe who turned all of Ulysses' shipmates into pigs.

Once Ulysses finally managed to make it back to Ithaca, nobody but his faithful dog recognized him. Dressed as a beggar, Ulysses discovered debauchery and hatred. His son Telemachus had grown into a young man, and his wife Penelope, convinced he was not coming home, was on the verge of marrying a new husband. Aided by Telemachus, who recognized him at last, Ulysses punished Penelope's suitors and won his dear wife back.

The Greek Gods

Comfortably settled at the top of mount Olympus, the twelve Greek Gods are ruled by their great leader Zeus, the master of lightening. Some—like Athena, the goddess of wisdom, and Poseidon, the god of the sea—liked to interfere with the lives of men and women on earth. (Both Athena and Poseidon played an important role in the Odyssey.)

The Age of Rome

Legend or reality? The history of Rome started in 753 BC when two twin brothers, Romulus and Remus, adopted and raised by a wolf, started a new city on the banks of the river Tiber. First governed by the Etruscan kings, Rome grew larger and stronger until it became a republic with modern institutions.

Hannibal,
Carthaginian general
(circa 247-183 BC)

Thanks to its large, well-trained army and the courage of its soldiers, Rome conquered all of Italy and Sicily. Rome also resisted attack from Hannibal, the king of Carthage, who had his elephants cross the Alps to fight.

In the first century BC, the powerful general, Julius Caesar, was at the peak of his power: he conquered Gaul and defeated all of his rivals. In 44 BC, shortly after he met the beautiful Cleopatra—the powerful pharaoh of Egypt—he was assassinated.

ANTOINE ET CLEOPATRE
ARS AMATORIA

Cleopatra later fell for Antony, another Roman general, and encouraged him to fight and win back his homeland. However, when he lost the battle of Actium, Antony killed himself. Cleopatra then killed herself by letting a snake bite her arm.

The Empire

For the first centuries of the modern age, Rome was the most powerful city in the world. With over one million inhabitants, the empire stretched from the North Sea to the Sahara, and from the Atlantic Ocean to the Black Sea! The Roman Empire marks the beginning of decadence. While their soldiers fought to keep the empire, Roman citizens cared mostly about two things: *panem et circenses,* Latin for "bread and circuses." The Colosseum, a massive amphitheater that sat up to 50,000 spectators, hosted regular gladiator battles. The first Christians were often persecuted, but in AD 313, the Emperor Constantine ordered the persecution to stop, allowing the new religion to advance in the "new Rome" of the east, the city of Constantinople.

The gladiators were often criminals or prisoners of war. With a net and a trident, the retiarius confronts the murmillo.

Under Constantine (circa AD 285-337), Christianity is brought to the empire.

A Gallic Feast

What a table! The Gallic people loved a good feast. They ate wild boar roasts, fish, and even snails and frogs. In Gaul, the culinary arts promised a great future for food in the region.

The Romans first called the Celts "Gallic"—meaning "cockerel"—to ridicule them. Loud, brash, and boastful, the Gallic always wanted to fight, even with each other.

With excellent artisans and skillful blacksmiths, their inventions would stand the test of time: the plough, the combine harvester, the barrel, the sickle, the rake, the wheel clad in iron, and even breeches, the ancestors of our modern pants.

Alesia

It was 52 BC. Roman troops under Julius Caesar invaded Gaul. The untiring Gallic soldiers of Alesia, a camp under the leadership of Vercingetorix, resisted the Roman invaders for as long as they could. After a long siege, Vercingetorix was forced to surrender. He left his weapons at the feet of Caesar, who later had him killed in a dingy Roman jail. Gaul then became a Roman province.

Jesus

THE DIVINE CHILD IS BORN.

Guided by a star, three wise men—Melchior, Caspar, and Balthazar—visit baby Jesus in a stable in Bethlehem. Joseph and Mary, the happy parents, raise their son as a carpenter, but soon realize a different destiny awaits him.

In Galilee, Jesus, along with his twelve disciples, spread the Gospel: the kingdom of God will soon come. The authorities disapprove the message, and Pontius Pilate, the Roman prosecutor, condemns Jesus to be crucified. Despite the efforts to ignore it, Jesus' message of love continued to spread all over the earth.

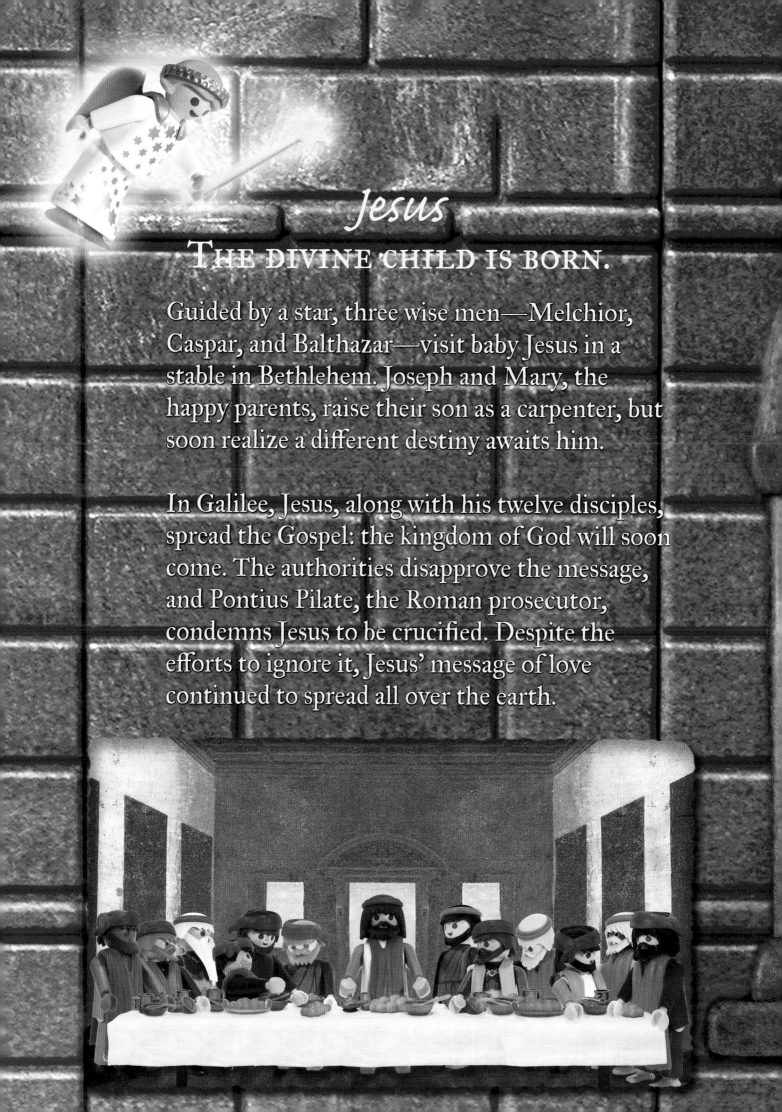

The Fascinating Middle Ages

The Middle Ages stretch from the fall of Rome in AD 476 to the start of the Renaissance in the 15th Century—a thousand years! The rich and turbulent history begins with the barbarian invasions of the Huns, Visigoths, and Vandals; continues with the birth of the Frankish kingdom; and starts to decline with the birth of the Carolingian Empire. Charlemagne, the emperor with the "flowery beard" whom the pope crowned on Christmas day in AD 800, dominates this period. During his reign, Europe rose from its ashes and began building for the future: roads opened; education became more widespread; stone buildings appeared; and artisans produced beautiful clothes, jewelry, and tapestries. Meanwhile, in the silence of the monasteries, monks diligently copied the Bible, as well as great texts of ancient times.

The Lady and The Unicorn, tapestry from the 15th Century.

In the Name of the Cross

In medieval Europe, the Christian church was everywhere. Some holy places are visited by pilgrims. Pilgrims, or "walkers of God" visit different places, such as Rome (Italy), Mont Saint-Michel (France), and Santiago de Compostela (Spain) to honor the relics of saints or places where miracles occurred.

At the end of the 11th Century, the pope commanded Christians to take back Jerusalem and the Holy Land from the Muslims who conquered it, marking the beginning of the crusades. These long military expeditions recruited thousands of men, from humble peasants to noble knights. Though bloody and cruel, the crusades introduced Eastern marvels to Europeans, such as the sultans' palaces and the magnificence of *One Thousand and One Nights*. In England, while Richard the Lion Heart was away on the crusades, usurpers tried to take over the throne. Luckily, Robin Hood and his Merry Men of Sherwood Forest were guarding it!

"Saladin" (1138-1193), the Sword of Islam, who conquered Jerusalem in 1187

Frederick Barbarossa, German Emperor (1122-1190)

Robin Hood (1160-1247)

Richard the Lion Heart (1157-1199)

Deep in the forest, a magic sword—Excalibur—was buried
in a rock. According to legend, only the one true king could
pull the sword from the stone. All of the noblest knights
tried, but failed. In the end, a young squire named Arthur
pulled out the sword, became king, and married the beautiful
Guinevere.

Merlin, a magician with extraordinary powers, gave King
Arthur a castle, Camelot, and a round table to gather the
noblest knights he could find. They would become the
Knights of the Round Table.

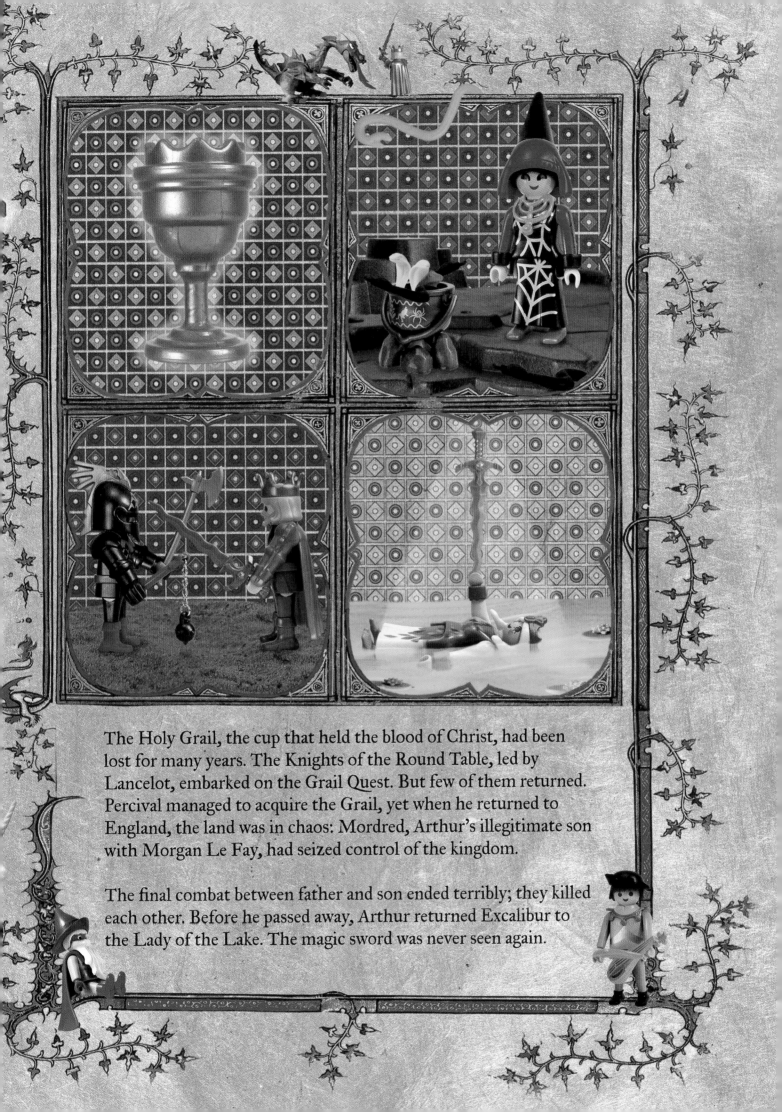

The Holy Grail, the cup that held the blood of Christ, had been
lost for many years. The Knights of the Round Table, led by
Lancelot, embarked on the Grail Quest. But few of them returned.
Percival managed to acquire the Grail, yet when he returned to
England, the land was in chaos: Mordred, Arthur's illegitimate son
with Morgan Le Fay, had seized control of the kingdom.

The final combat between father and son ended terribly; they killed
each other. Before he passed away, Arthur returned Excalibur to
the Lady of the Lake. The magic sword was never seen again.

Muhammad:
THE BIRTH OF ISLAM

In the beginning of the 7th century in
the deserts of Arabia, Muhammad was
a prosperous 40-year-old camel driver.
Muhammad often retreated to the cave
of Hira to meditate. One night, when
Muhammad had fallen asleep, the angel
Gabriel, shining with light, awoke him
with these words:

"You are God's emissary,
Allah's prophet."

A new religion was born from the revelation: Islam.

The Vikings

Vikings braved the Northern seas in
their magnificent *drekars*, or ships.
Shortly before the year 1000,
Erik the Red was banished
from Iceland.

With a few crew members, this courageous sailor set course
for the West. He discovered a frozen land, which he ironically
named Greenland to attract many settlers!

A few years later, Leif Erikson, son of Erik, also took to the
sea, heading to the West. The Viking discovered new lands and
extraordinary new cultures. Without knowing it, he reached the
land that, 500 years later, would be named North America.

1066. On his deathbed, King Edward of England bequeathed his throne to his cousin William, Duke of Normandy.

The traitor Harold instea‹ crowned himself king.

William's fleet crossed the English Channel.

At the Battle of **Hastings,** Harold's army was torn to pieces. Harold was mortally wounded by an arr›

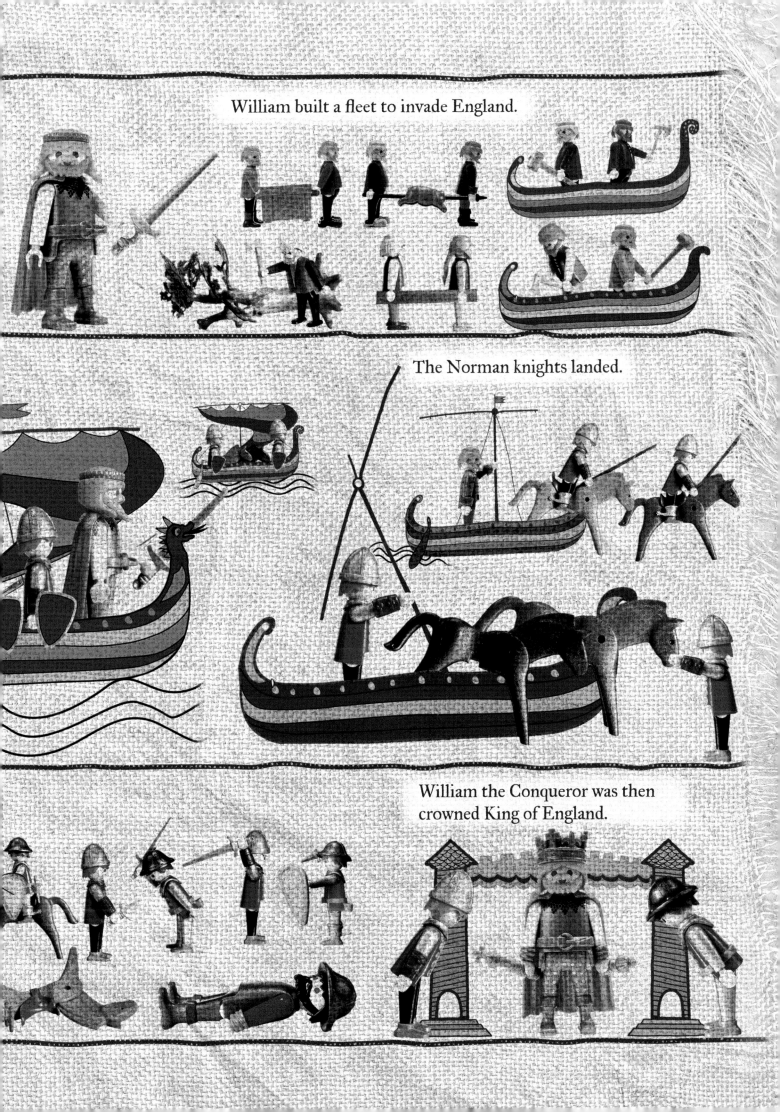

William built a fleet to invade England.

The Norman knights landed.

William the Conqueror was then crowned King of England.

Jousting

To protect themselves against invasions and raids, nobles built magnificent fortified castles on high ground. Security features included moats, thick defensive walls, high towers, and a drawbridge.

THE DAWN OF HISTORY

Jousting tournaments proved one's value, dexterity, and bravery. Armed from head to toe, and wearing the colors of their lord, the knights waited impatiently for their turn to join in the jousting.

In the gallery, Lady Eleanor raises her hand, signaling the start! The two competing knights race towards each other for the first assault.

Penitence! Penitence!

"Pray, good people, as the Apocalypse and the Day of Reckoning are at hand!"

In 1347, the plague arrived in the port of Genoa. Princes and valets, monks, beggars, and knights all die in terrible agony—no one is spared from disease.

The Plague

Covered in large black boils, the plague-stricken patients suffered from inflamed throats and lungs, and would often vomit blood. It took less than a week for the infected to die, abandoned by their family and friends who fled from contamination. Chaos spread across Europe! Cities were deserted. The monks prayed, fasted, and lashed themselves in penance, but nothing stopped the epidemic; in only 50 years, a third of the Christian world died from the Plague.

Joan of Arc Frees Orleans

Joan and the King

Saint Catherine

Joan of Arc was a young French shepherdess from Lorraine. One day, as her sheep were grazing, three saints appeared to her—St. Michael, St. Catherine, and St. Margaret—instructing her to chase the English out of France. Joan went to see King Charles VII to pass on the divine message.

When the king finally granted her an audience, he hid among his courtiers and asked a noble lord to pretend to be him on the throne. But St. Michael, St. Catherine, and St. Margaret warned Joan of the trick and led her to King Charles.

The brave Joan asked the king to provide her with an army in order to rid Orleans of the English.

Joan at the Stake

Resting after the battle

Joan at the doors of Paris

Pierre Cauchon

Charles VII, convinced by the young girl, gave her an army, a sword, some armor, and a flag. Joan lead an army of brutes and mercenaries, and won their respect. Tough knights like Cahire, the Duke of Alençon, and Gilles de Rais even became her comrades-in-arms. As the saints foretold, Joan freed Orleans on May 8th, 1429, and had Charles VII crowned in Reims on July 17th.

After a few more successful wins, Joan's luck turned. She was captured outside Compiègne. During her trial, Bishop Pierre Cauchon, secret ally to the English, accused her of being a witch—a crime punishable by death! Joan was found guilty and executed in Rouen on May 30th, 1431.

Joan

Saint Margret

Marco Polo
Meets Kublai Khan

In the 13th century, after a four-year journey through Asia, the young Venetian merchant Marco Polo met the Emperor of China, Kublai Khan. For over twenty years, Marco Polo served in Khan's court, traveling across the vast empire and discovering its marvels.

When he returned to Venice, Marco told about the thousand palaces covered with gold, carts made of silk, fantastic animals, noodles, and even paper money! Unfortunately nobody believed him. In 1298 he wrote *The Travels of Marco Polo* to detail his experiences. Two centuries later, this book inspired an eager reader—Christopher Columbus.

The Earth is round—everyone knows that. But in the 15th century, no one believed it. But Christopher Columbus did. He persuaded the King and Queen of Spain to give him three boats to find a route to China and India by traveling west rather than east.

1492. After a long journey across the ocean, Columbus's ship reached land. Columbus was convinced he had arrived in India. But the gold, the palaces, the spices, and the silk described by Marco Polo were nowhere to be found. Instead there were unknown things like cocoa, coffee, tobacco, rubber, corn, hammocks, and strange animals.

Later, people realized this country on the other side of the Atlantic was not China or India, but rather a new continent— a "new world!"

Leonardo da Vinci was a genius, an artist, and an inventor with a brilliant imagination. He was born in 1452, the middle of the Italian Renaissance, in the small town of Vinci, not far from Florence. Leonardo protected the secrets of his discoveries by writing his notes from right to left, so only he could read them in front of a mirror. Leonardo made countless sketches, hoping to discover the secrets of the world. His wildest dream was to invent a machine that could fly.

Leonardo conducted lots of optical experiments. He built a camera obscura ("dark room," in Latin), a device with which he was able to capture landscapes. Leonardo was the first to observe the similarities between the way the camera obscura and the human eye worked.

Leonardo was also an ingenious military engineer:

He imagined a cannon with multiple barrels.

He drew a huge crossbow pulled by horses.

The Queen of the Seas

Elizabeth, the daughter of Henry VIII (the English King known for his six wives) loved to dress in extravagant clothes, pearls, and other luxurious jewelry. Intelligent and powerful, she turned England into a wealthy and mighty country.

Francis Drake, a daring sailor and the Queen's favorite admiral, completed the second circumnavigation of the globe and seized control of California. Drake's mission was to protect England from the Spanish. In 1588, he sank 28 Spanish ships of the "Invincible Armada" in a single day.

Elizabeth, an Anglican, fought against both the Catholics and the Protestants and survived many plots against her.

Mary Stuart, Queen of Scotland—Elizabeth's cousin—claimed she should be Queen of England. Elizabeth locked Mary up and then beheaded her in the terrible Tower of London in 1588. A Shakespearean tragedy!

Under the reign of Elizabeth I, England became a maritime power renowned across the whole of Europe.

At Shakespeare's Theater

We know surprisingly little about the life of William Shakespeare, the genius author from England of the late 16th and early 17th century. So little, in fact, that some people don't think he wrote all of his plays! This is of very little importance—his plays still delight audiences across the world today.

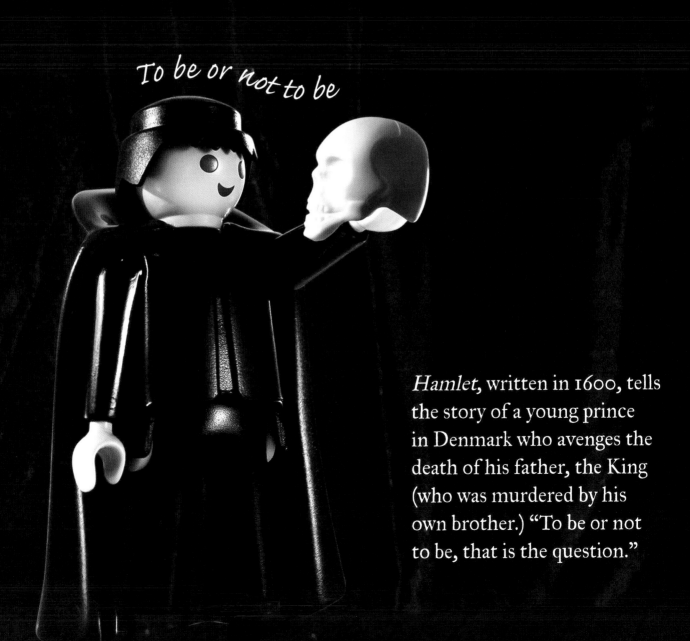

To be or not to be

Hamlet, written in 1600, tells the story of a young prince in Denmark who avenges the death of his father, the King (who was murdered by his own brother.) "To be or not to be, that is the question."

Romeo and Juliet is a beautiful love story that ends in tragedy. Set in Verona, Italy, two young people fall in love, but their families, the Montagues and the Capulets, hate each other deeply. The family feud prevents the pair from marrying. The young couple chooses death rather than renounce their passion.

Galileo Reaches for the Stars

On January 7, 1610, Galileo looked toward the moon with his extraordinary new invention, the telescope.

In just one night of looking to the sky, a thousand years of beliefs were shaken. The moon wasn't a smooth, perfect sphere made of polished crystal. It was an uneven ball, covered with craters, valleys, and mountains. Galileo was shocked by his discovery.

Night after night, he pointed his telescope up to the stars. He discovered that the Milky Way was not a trail of milk sprung from the bosom of a divine force, but actually a gigantic ensemble of billions of stars. He discovered that four moons circled Jupiter, just like the moon circled Earth. After all of his discoveries, Galileo believed that the sun—not Earth—was at the center of the universe, like Copernicus before him.

The church, however, did not believe this theory. In 1633, the church condemned the scientist, forcing him to recant.

Town Market

Merchants and street vendors gather in town to sell their goods. While
the fishmonger smokes his trout, the butcher prepares his meat, the
market-gardener displays his fresh products, and the miller takes out
his bags of flour. In his study, a trader writes a bill of sale. On the
cathedral terrace, the vicar and the canon watch the circus and the
merry band of musicians. Old women gossip, students relax between
Latin lessons, scoundrels pick pockets, and beggars ask for money.

In Versailles, Louis XIV welcomes an ambassador from the East.

The whole court—the Sun King's family, his minister Colbert, a troop of musketeers, dukes in wigs and beautiful powdered marquises—gathered in front of the palace.

After exchanging gifts, they take a walk around the splendid gardens of the castle before heading to a dance in the Hall of Mirrors. Afterwards, it's time to laugh at the royal theatre: Molière's latest comedy is being performed and La Fontaine is reciting some of his fables. The age of Louis XIV really was a Great Century!

The Magic Flute (1791) is an opera by Mozart. It is a w

The wise Sarastro, the Great Master of the Sun, helps the

accompanied by Papageno

only with a magic flute.

a bird catcher dressed in feathers. After many

Sei standhaft, duldsam und verschwiegen, kurz, sei ein Mann

Papagena meine schöne

Papagena.

Pamina meets his lover. Papagena

Pamina and Papageno

The Magic Flute by Mozart

tale whose heavenly music has spanned the centuries.

mino deliver Princess Pamina from the clutches of her possessive mother,

the Queen of the Night. In order to defeat the dragons, Tamino

Mutiny on the Bounty

Pacific Ocean, April 1789.

It had been a year since the Bounty left England on its mission to bring back exotic plants from Tahiti. Captain Bligh, tyrannical and cruel, never shied away from whipping his men. Some say he even threw sailors overboard.

The men of the Bounty stayed on the island for six months to collect precious plants. The native Vahines were welcoming, the fruits were ripe with sun, and the fish tasted delicious. The sailors didn't want to return to the fog of London!

On the journey back, a mutiny broke out. Led by Lieutenant Fletcher Christian, the sailors of the Bounty left Captain Bligh and a few of his followers on a lifeboat in the middle of the Pacific Ocean. They threw the exotic plants overboard and sailed back to their Tahitian fiancées.

As for Captain Bligh, though he was cruel, he was an exceptionally talented sailor; he managed to cross the Pacific aboard his small lifeboat.

July 14th, 1789

"We will make it happen..." sing the Parisians. On this day, the French Revolution began. The people stormed the fortress of the Bastille in the heart of Paris. In short, the kingdom of France was thrown into chaos. The rights of the noblemen and the clergy were abolished and the rights of every citizen were asserted. Soon after, the king was sent to the guillotine.

Vive la République!

Napoléon (1769-1821)
EMPEROR OF THE FRENCH

To some a fierce dictator, to others the architect of revolution, and to everyone a strategic genius, Napoléon, a short Corsican standing at only 5 feet 3 inches tall, became a general at 25, a consul at 30, and Emperor at 35.

There are many different opinions of the Emperor. He modernized the institutions of France and created the Civil and Penal Codes, the laws that govern the
day-to-day lives of the people. But at the same time, hundreds of thousands of lives
were lost because of his pursuit of power and glory.

Abukir, Austerlitz, Trafalgar, Jena, Eylau, Friedland,
Wagram, Moscow, Berezina, Waterloo...

There are as many battlegrounds as
there are huge cemeteries.

The Wreck of the Medusa

In 1816, the Medusa sank in the middle of the Atlantic Ocean due to an incompetent captain. Some survivors of the wreckage took shelter on a raft and drifted for several weeks off the coast of Africa, without food or water and in a shark-infested sea.

Three years later, the painter Géricault immortalized the moment when the survivors caught sight of the boat that would rescue them. One must always have hope, even in the darkest of moments: this seems to be the lesson of the painting.

The Imaginary Museum

Since the age of cavemen, humans have loved painting the world around them and recreating their history through pictures.
In the 19th century, the major cities in Europe created public museums so that everyone could admire great art: the Louvre in Paris, the British Museum in London, the Prado in Madrid...

From the secrecy of their workshops, painters aim to immortalize the world around them: Goya pays tribute to the Spanish shot by Napoleon's soldiers, and Delacroix paints Liberty Leading the People in Paris in 1830. Other artists prefer to take their easels outside: Vincent van Gogh paints sunflowers and Claude Monet the water lilies of his garden. As for Henri Rousseau, he just lets his imagination run wild!

Eugène Delacroix
(1798-1863)

Vincent Van Gogh
(1853-1890)

Claude Monet
(1840-1926)

Henri Rousseau
(1844-1910)

Traveling up the Mississippi

In the 19th century, millions of Europeans come to settle the huge American continent. The pioneers head west, trying to conquer this vast land. They discover a wild place inhabited by eagles, beavers, bears, and buffaloes. The trappers that follow the rivers encounter the Native American tribes: the two cultures get to know each other, for better or worse...

The Birth of a Nation

The history of the United States is fairly recent, but what a history it is! In the Wild West, it was the law of the gun that decided the fate of the most powerful country in the world.

The Conquest of the West

Americans declared their independence on July 4, 1776. The growing number of settlers pushed the Native Americans onto territories, despite resistance from the Sioux and the Apaches.

The Gold Rush of 1848 inspired a taste for adventure. It was the age of cowboys, wagons, saloons, bandits, and sheriffs. You had to know how to handle your money and a horse in order to protect your family.

WANTED

BILLY THE KID

WANTED

PAT GARRETT

JESSIE JAMES
1000 $

DENVER ST. LOUIS

TERN EXPRESS

THE UNITED STATES OF AM

5

7 G

G 06714289 *

7

FREE

5

United States Divided

The rich and industrial Northern states fight the pro-slavery, agricultural states of the South. It is the American Civil War (1861-1865).

Led by President Lincoln and General Grant, the Northern Yankees defeat the Southern Confederates, led by General Lee. Slavery is abolished and millions of former slaves taste freedom.

The Modern Age

Here comes the 20th century! Genius inventors revolutionize people's daily lives. Thanks to Graham Bell's invention of the telephone, people can talk to each other from thousands of miles apart. Thomas Edison's light bulb fills the night with light, as if by magic. With their noise and their smoke, the first cars scare everyone. But people quickly get used to these four-wheeled machines, and the cars themselves soon become faster and much more comfortable. Before long, they are indispensable! Then comes the time of moving pictures. After Niepce and Daguerre invent photography, Lumière then creates cinematography. All the adventures of the world are paraded in motion before astonished eyes. The invention of cinema is perhaps the greatest cultural revolution of the 20th century, creating immortal stars. In the kingdom of movies, the capital city is Hollywood, a place often known as "the dream factory."

Graham Bell (1847-1922), the inventor of the telephone.

Thomas Edison (1847-1931). Edison invented, among other things, the electric lightbulb.

DU 17 AU 27 OCTOBRE 1913
XIVᵉ EXPOSITION INTERNATIONALE
DE L'AUTOMOBILE

Grand Palais - Champs Elysées - Paris

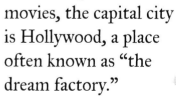

The Interpretation of Dreams by Sigmund Freud

Let's Dream a Little

Dreams, what are they all about? In Vienna, a doctor named Sigmund Freud considered a beautiful puzzle, why do we dream? And what do dreams mean in the silence of the night? His work with his patients gives birth to a new kind of science: psychoanalysis, the study of the most secret corners of our minds. Freud's theories influence scientists, but also poets, writers, painters, and musicians. In the '20s and '30s, in Europe, the Surrealist movement got rid of the constraints of reality; instead, it made way for the imagination and the surprising associations between words and pictures, such as in the works of Salvador Dali. Meanwhile, America also moves forward with the birth of Jazz, a new music that celebrates improvisation and rhythm. Following the sound of the piano, trumpet, and saxophone, Duke Ellington, Louis Armstrong, and Sydney Bechet make our hearts sing and our legs dance.

Marc Chagall (1887-1985)

Thanks to the protests of British and American suffragettes, women win the right to vote in the 20th century.

The Scientists

Continuing the work of the 19th century, scientists revolutionize their fields and invent the modern age.

Charles Darwin (1809 - 1882) discovers that humans and monkeys have a common ancestor, and that all animal species evolve due to natural selection. His theories cause uproar as they question the Biblical creation story of Adam and Eve.

Louis Pasteur (1822-1895) discovers a vaccine to prevent rabies. He also discovers how to pasteurize food, allowing people to consume food and drink free from germs. When you drink milk in the morning, you have Louis Pasteur to thank!

Rontgen (1845-1923) discovers X-rays, which allow doctors to take pictures of what's inside the body. This can also help surgeons find their scalpels in case they ever forget them inside a patient!

Marie Curie (1867-1934) discovers a highly radioactive metal: radium. For her work, she is the first woman in history to receive a Nobel Prize.

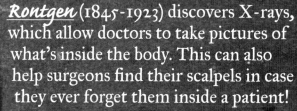

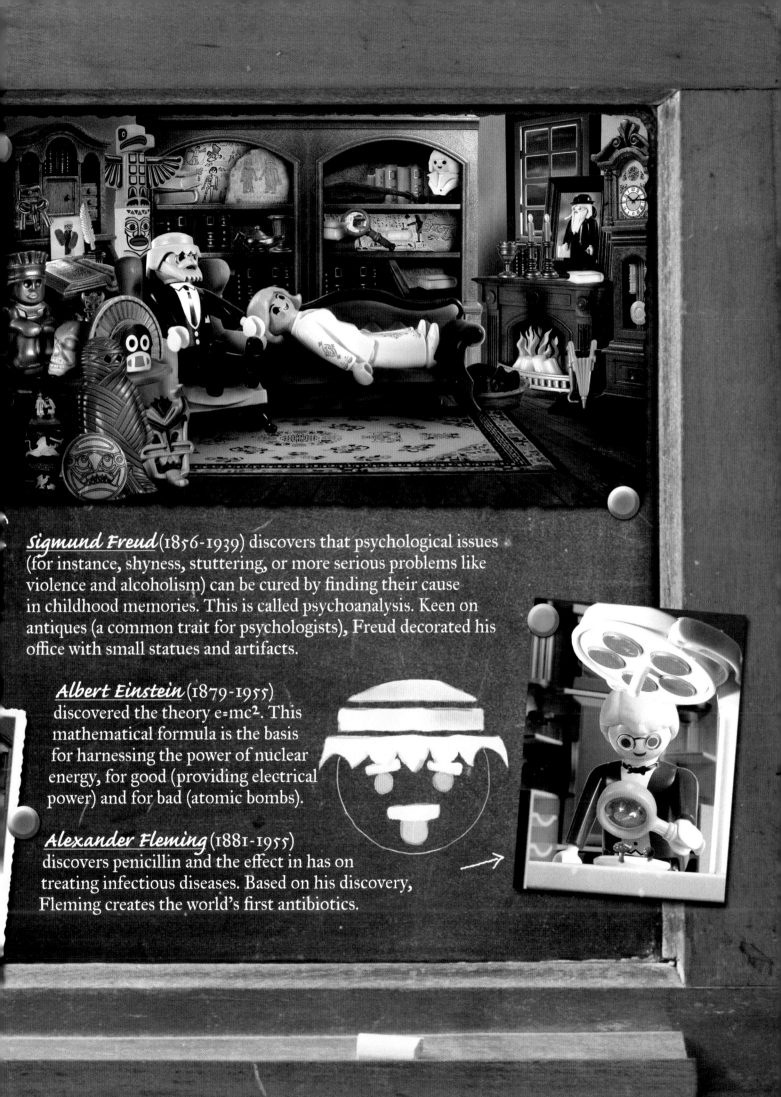

Sigmund Freud (1856-1939) discovers that psychological issues (for instance, shyness, stuttering, or more serious problems like violence and alcoholism) can be cured by finding their cause in childhood memories. This is called psychoanalysis. Keen on antiques (a common trait for psychologists), Freud decorated his office with small statues and artifacts.

Albert Einstein (1879-1955) discovered the theory e=mc². This mathematical formula is the basis for harnessing the power of nuclear energy, for good (providing electrical power) and for bad (atomic bombs).

Alexander Fleming (1881-1955) discovers penicillin and the effect in has on treating infectious diseases. Based on his discovery, Fleming creates the world's first antibiotics.

Faster, Further

As long as we have existed, humans have loved to travel. Their legs, their animals, and the wind provided power for thousands of years. At the end of the 19th century, and in the beginning of the 20th, it's time to move up...

It's the AGE OF MACHINES!

In the space of a few short years, there was a true revolution. Powered by enormous steam engines, trains began to cross continents. On the seas, old sailboats made way for huge iron giants. Everybody wanted to board the Titanic, launched with great celebration in 1912. Its tragic sinking didn't stop new models from being built—always bigger, always faster, always more luxurious.

Lastly, the incredible adventure of aviation! Starting in 1903, with the first flight of the Wright brothers, the technology moves forward each year in giant steps. What a huge journey between the fragile early propeller aircraft and today's supersonic jets! An age-old human dream has more than come true; we are able to fly higher and faster than the birds, even into the immensity of space.

It all begins in Sarajevo, Bosnia. On June 28, 1914, the heir to the throne of the Austrian Empire is assassinated in his carriage. Within a few weeks, the whole of Europe is mobilized for conflict.

In Berlin, soldiers head off to war enthusiastically: they think it will be a very quick battle. What a mistake! World War I will last four years and kill over 10 million people.

World War I will drag old Europe through terrible changes. In October 1917, a communist revolution takes place in Russia, leading to many years of suffering under a terrible dictatorship.

Germany's fate is even worse; by 1933, it has chosen cruel monsters as its leaders. Night falls upon Europe. From 1939 to 1945, World War II takes place, and is even more terrible and cruel than the first. And, for many reasons, its story cannot be told here and we will keep a respectful silence.

Though it is an era of progress, the 20th century is also stained by apocalyptic wars. This is what civilization can become if the worst side of humanity takes over. We must always stay alert!

Civilians will always pay a higher price than the animals responsible for war and cruelty. It is civilians who will flee their native countries, the villages where they grew up, and move as far away as possible from the people who want to harm them.

Finally, in 1945, the United Nations (UN) is created in order for the world to work together for peace. People of colors, all nations, and all beliefs are meant to live together!

July 21, 1969

The world holds its breath: the first man sets foot on the Moon! "It's one small step for man, one giant leap for mankind," Neil Armstrong exclaims as he first steps on the Moon. Meanwhile, on Earth, the hippies invent a new way of life. It's time for cultural and moral freedom, for bright colors and pop music:
"Make love, not war!"

A Crazy, Crazy World

We hurry, honk, buzz, ring, phone, surf, chat, go traveling, take pictures, work, sell, wait, buy, consume, enjoy, drive, pollute, waste, meet one another, love one another, fly away, split up, walk, run, cycle, fight, make films, throw things away, make things dirty, clean things up, make choices, vote, change our minds, have a laugh... In short, we are alive.

And Tomorrow?

Tomorrow, or at least soon, we will see many more changes; maybe we will go for vacations on different planets or into other solar systems!

Welcome to the Cosmos Fun Park, the first interplanetary resort for family holidays!

The program includes: guided tours, meeting friendly aliens, discovering the local gastronomy, trips to a nearby asteroid, space-scooter rides, exotic experiences, and getting tanned under the stars...

Bring on tomorrow!

Grazie

To Frank and David Fellous, Fabienne Maillet, Nicolas Boen, and Bernard Benayoun for the assistance they provided from the very beginning right up to the completion of this book. To Gaël Baudouin, the tower that checkmates me.

A huge thank you and all my gratitude to Jean-Louis Michaud-Soret for his support, his advice, and his encouragement, as well as Muriel Zammit, Bruno Berrard, Laurent Lafay, and the entire dream team from Evry.

To all my friends, thank you for your infallible enthusiasm: Thomas Bonnin, Franck Tusolini, Emmanuel Zini, Laetitia Paoli, Lolo "la Muella," Muriel Sadoun, Patrick Bonnard, Jennifer and Raphaël Lerner, JMS, Nancy Danino, Gwendoline Malrieu, Séverine Yvan and Igor Chometowski, Antoine Amselem, Liza Korn, Antoinette Merlin and everyone from her "Nakin Club's Band," Emilie and Ghislain, Stéphanie and Blaise, Hervech "the Beast," Sylvain Tusolini, Bénédicte, Dorothée, Pauline, and Clémence. And a thousand thanks to Estelle.

To my grandfather Yankel, to my parents, Charly and Alex, and to my sister, Sandy, thanks to whom I am an artist. To Nicole and Michel Slotine and all their marvelous friends. To my bros and sis, who provide me with Playmobil pieces: Max Scher, Élie Partouche, Gary, Océano, and Jordan, Arthur Dupont, and above all to Sarah Paquet, great collector of Playmobil. To Andrés Marty, to Michael Skornik, to Mrs. Le Mee, Sandrine Martin and their colleagues from Yvelines, to Marianne Cohen and Richard Sebban for their temporary yet very productive help. Special thanks to Jean-Michel Coblence for his pugnacity and his adventurous spirit.

All my affectionate and eternal gratitude to my masters and teachers: Isabelle Clark and Daniel Costelle, Mrs. Borée, Raphaël Cohen, Xavier Ramet, and Messrs. Giovaccini, Msika, Duong, Remoissenet, Tarnowsky, but also to Albert Barillé and Alain Decaux.

And a thousand thanks to my Mac, a million of thanks to Calliope.

For Judith, thanks to Judith.

By the same author...

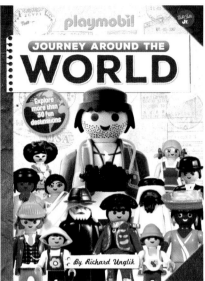

Quarto is the authority on a wide range of topics.
Quarto educates, entertains, and enriches the lives of our readers—
enthusiasts and lovers of hands-on living.
www.quartoknows.com

6 Orchard Road, Suite 100
Lake Forest, CA 92630
quartoknows.com
Visit our blogs @quartoknows.com

Translated by Marion Serre.

© 2016 by geobra Brandstätter Stiftung & Co. KG, Zirndorf/Germany
® PLAYMOBIL pronounced: plāy - mō - bēēl
www.playmobil.com
licensed by: BAVARIA MEDIA, www.bavaria-media.de

© Casterman, 2011
www.casterman.com

Casterman Editions
47 Cantersteen, boite 4
1000 Bruxelles

Printed in China
10 9 8 7 6 5 4 3 2 1

To Frank and David Fellous, Fabienne Maillet, Nicolas Boen, and Bernard Benayoun for the assistance they provided from the very beginning right up to the completion of this book. To Gaël Baudouin, the tower that checkmates me.

A huge thank you and all my gratitude to Jean-Louis Michaud-Soret for his support, his advice, and his encouragement, as well as Muriel Zammit, Bruno Berrard, Laurent Lafay, and the entire dream team from Evry.

To all my friends, thank you for your infallible enthusiasm: Thomas Bonnin, Franck Tusolini, Emmanuel Zini, Laetitia Paoli, Lolo "la Muella," Muriel Sadoun, Patrick Bonnard, Jennifer and Raphaël Lerner, JMS, Nancy Danino, Gwendoline Malrieu, Séverine Yvan and Igor Chometowski, Antoine Amselem, Liza Korn, Antoinette Merlin and everyone from her "Nakin Club's Band," Emilie and Ghislain, Stéphanie and Blaise, Hervech "the Beast," Sylvain Tusolini, Bénédicte, Dorothée, Pauline, and Clémence. And a thousand thanks to Estelle.

To my grandfather Yankel, to my parents, Charly and Alex, and to my sister, Sandy, thanks to whom I am an artist. To Nicole and Michel Slotine and all their marvelous friends. To my bros and sis, who provide me with Playmobil pieces: Max Scher, Élie Partouche, Gary, Océano, and Jordan, Arthur Dupont, and above all to Sarah Paquet, great collector of Playmobil. To Andrés Marty, to Michael Skornik, to Mrs. Le Mee, Sandrine Martin and their colleagues from Yvelines, to Marianne Cohen and Richard Sebban for their temporary yet very productive help. Special thanks to Jean-Michel Coblence for his pugnacity and his adventurous spirit.

All my affectionate and eternal gratitude to my masters and teachers: Isabelle Clark and Daniel Costelle, Mrs. Borée, Raphaël Cohen, Xavier Ramet, and Messrs. Giovaccini, Msika, Duong, Remoissenet, Tarnowsky, but also to Albert Barillé and Alain Decaux.

And a thousand thanks to my Mac, a million of thanks to Calliope.

For Judith, thanks to Judith.

By the same author...

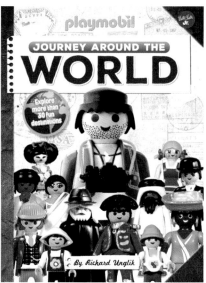

Quarto is the authority on a wide range of topics.
Quarto educates, entertains, and enriches the lives of our readers—
enthusiasts and lovers of hands-on living.
www.quartoknows.com

6 Orchard Road, Suite 100
Lake Forest, CA 92630
quartoknows.com
Visit our blogs @quartoknows.com

Translated by Marion Serre.

© 2016 by geobra Brandstätter Stiftung & Co. KG, Zirndorf/Germany
® PLAYMOBIL pronounced: plāy - mō - bēel
www.playmobil.com
licensed by: BAVARIA MEDIA, www.bavaria-media.de

© Casterman, 2011
www.casterman.com

Casterman Editions
47 Cantersteen, boite 4
1000 Bruxelles

Printed in China
10 9 8 7 6 5 4 3 2 1